JESU, JOY OF MAN'S L

Chorale from Cantata Nº 147

Arranged for piano duet
by Myra Hess

J. S. BACH

OXFORD UNIVERSITY PRESS, MUSIC DEPARTMENT, WALTON STREET, OXFORD OX2 6DP

'Jesu, Joy of Man's Desiring' is the first line of an original poem by the late Robert Bridges and is used by permission.

The cover reproduces in facsimile the first thirteen bars of this movement of Bach's autograph manuscript. This autograph is in the possession of the Staatsbibliothek (Preussischer Kulturbesitz), Musikabteilung, Berlin, by whose kind permission it is reproduced.

p
mf cant.
Ped. Ped. etc.
Ped.
p
p

p ma cantando
pp
non cant.
Ped.

poco f
Ped.
f
mf

decresc.
decresc.
mp
mf
(off)
Ped.

OXFORD UNIVERSITY PRESS
Reproduced and printed by
Halstan & Co. Ltd., Amersham, Bucks., England